LONDON

Richard Platt

Illustrated by Manuela Cappon

KINGFISHER

NEW YORK

London

In modern, noisy London, English words are everywhere, but each speaker sounds different. Visitors are baffled by native London words, but there's no mistaking the American accent of a group of businessmen in an upscale restaurant. Their waitress speaks perfect English but with an accent from elsewhere in Europe, and an Asian accent echoes from the kitchen. After all, London is not only the capital of Great Britain. It is the center of the English-speaking world and a flourishing European city.

Scotland

Glasgow   EDINBURGH

North Sea

Northern Ireland

BELFAST   UNITED KINGDOM

Atlantic Ocean

Irish Sea

REPUBLIC OF IRELAND

DUBLIN   Liverpool   Leeds

Manchester

England

Birmingham

Wales

CARDIFF   Bristol

LONDON

English Channel

FRANCE

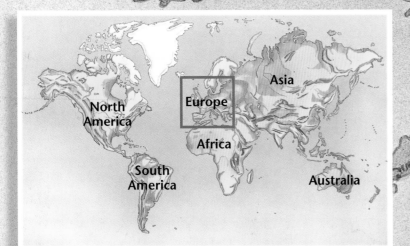

Asia

Europe

North America

Africa

South America

Australia

Throughout its long history, London has always been a place where people have met, mixed, and mingled. Spreading across a winding river on an island in the corner of Europe, the city first prospered almost 2,000 years ago. Success attracted jealous and greedy rivals and invaders intent on either conquering or destroying the city.

Over the centuries, Great Britain won empires in North America, Africa, and Asia. London thrived with each conquest. As each empire crumbled, London also declined—but never too far. In the 1900s, the city survived economic disaster, wartime bombs, and terrorist attacks. Today, it is looking toward a brighter future once again.

London in the A.D. 2000s

London timeline

300,000 B.C. Ice grips Great Britain: glaciers block the River Thames, forcing it southward to where it flows today

50,000 B.C. Hunters chase woolly mammoths and rhinoceros along the banks of the Thames

3500 B.C. Using stone axes, families fell trees on the banks of the Thames; they build a village

1100 B.C. The riverbank dwellers honor water gods by casting their finest bronze tools into the Thames

800 B.C. Celtic people from central Europe settle beside the Thames

A.D. 43 An invading Roman army bridges the Thames and lays the first stones of a new town, Londinium

A.D. 60 Led by the warrior-queen Boudicca, Celts destroy Londinium

A.D. 225 Romans surround their rebuilt city with a defensive wall

A.D. 407 Romans abandon Londinium

A.D. 500 Saxon people from Germany have started a new town, Lundenwic, to the west of the old walled city

A.D. 851 Danish Vikings attack Lundenwic; more raids follow

A.D. 1078 Norman duke William the Conqueror orders a tower (castle) built in London after capturing the city, and all of England, 12 years previously

A.D. 1209 A stone bridge across the Thames replaces earlier wooden ones

A.D. 1348 One-third of Londoners die as the Black Death infects the city

A.D. 1476 William Caxton begins to print books at Westminster

A.D. 1599 William Shakespeare's company of actors builds the Globe theater on the Thames's south bank

A.D. 1649 King Charles I is executed as civil war tears England apart

A.D. 1660 Londoner Samuel Pepys starts a diary that will make him famous

A.D. 1666 Fire destroys almost all the buildings within London's walls

A.D. 1675 Work begins on the rebuilding of St. Paul's Cathedral

A.D. 1809 First gas lamps light the streets

A.D. 1825 London becomes the largest city in the world

A.D. 1851 London hosts the Great Exhibition in Hyde Park

A.D. 1863 First underground trains run

A.D. 1940 World War II bombings destroy London buildings but kill few

A.D. 2005 London is selected to host the Summer Olympic Games in 2012

What do these dates mean?

B.C. means "before Christ." For example, 100 B.C. refers to 100 years before the birth of Jesus Christ, as traditionally calculated.

A.D. means "anno Domini" (medieval Latin for "year of our Lord") and refers to all dates after the birth of Christ.

300,000 B.C.

50,000 B.C.

1000 B.C.

A.D. 1

A.D. 100

A.D. 500

A.D. 1000

A.D. 1500

A.D. 2000

DENMARK

North Sea

Hamburg

NETHERLANDS

AMSTERDAM

THE HAGUE

Rotterdam

BELGIUM

GERMANY

BRUSSELS

Cologne

Bonn

Frankfurt

LUXEMBOURG

PARIS

Contents

The pages that follow trace London's long, dramatic history. Reading them, you will see how it was once just a riverside camp and later became a thriving town. You will discover how it was conquered and burned to the ground. And you will witness London flourishing once again, growing into a large, prosperous, multicultural city.

A Viking raid
page 14

Boudicca attacks!
page 10

Bridge of stone
page 18

Neolithic camp
page 6

Imperial supercity
page 12

London in A.D. 43

Fleet River
Walbrook Stream

N

Today's London
London A.D. 43
River Thames

A locator map shows how the city is growing over time and where each scene takes place.

Roman invasion
page 8

Norman London
page 16

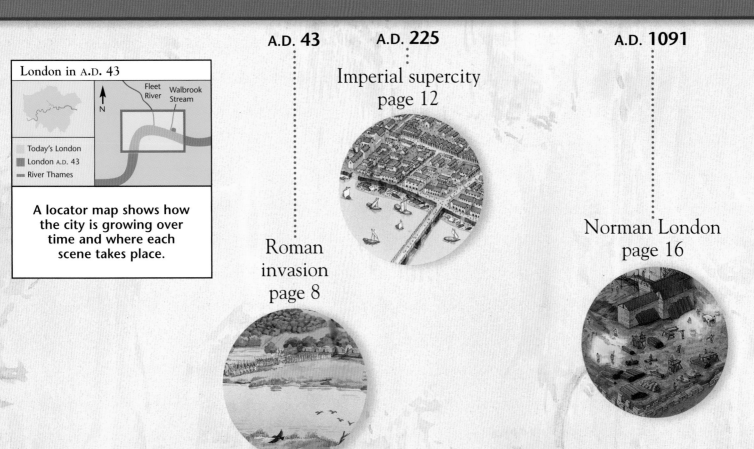

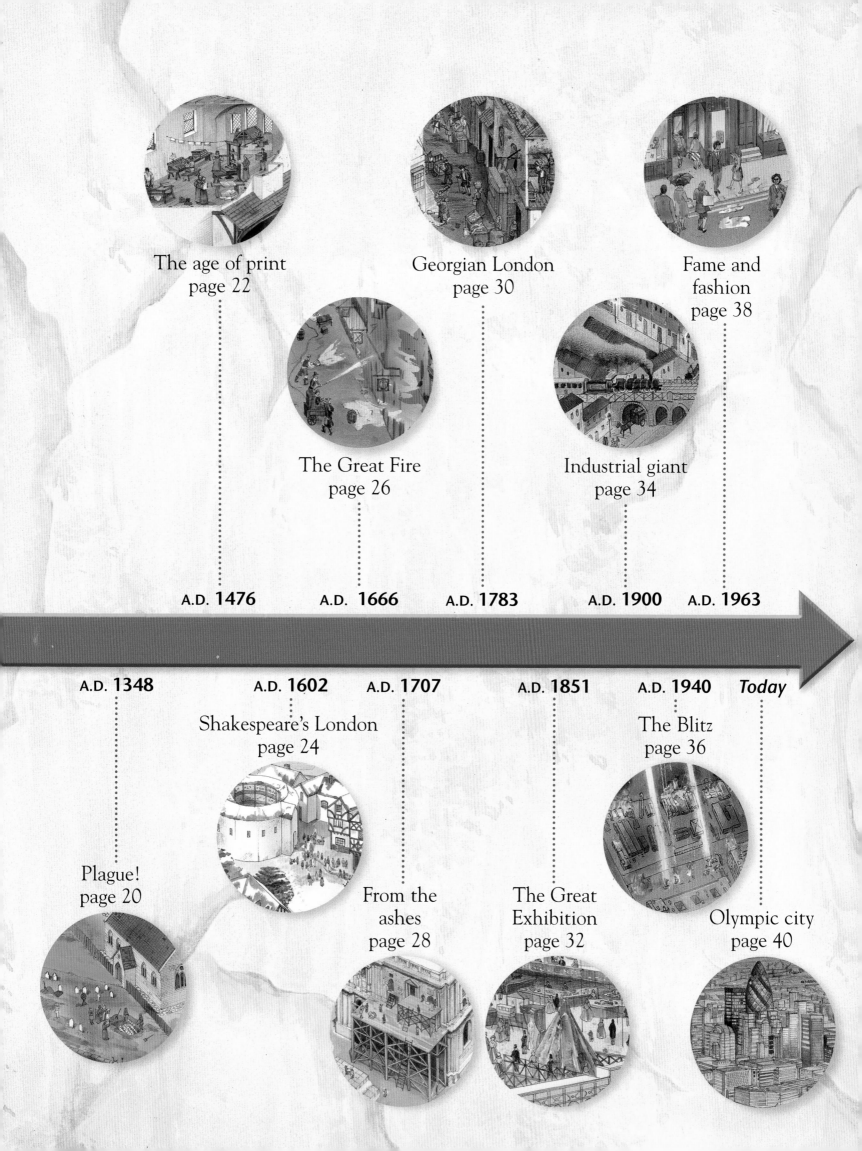

The age of print
page 22

Georgian London
page 30

Fame and
fashion
page 38

The Great Fire
page 26

Industrial giant
page 34

A.D. **1476**   A.D. **1666**   A.D. **1783**   A.D. **1900**   A.D. **1963**

A.D. **1348**   A.D. **1602**   A.D. **1707**   A.D. **1851**   A.D. **1940**   *Today*

Shakespeare's London
page 24

The Blitz
page 36

Plague!
page 20

From the
ashes
page 28

The Great
Exhibition
page 32

Olympic city
page 40

Neolithic camp 3500 B.C.

On a low, muddy bank in the middle of the shallow, winding River Thames, stealthy hunters hurl stone-tipped spears at a group of plump geese. But the geese fly off, honking with alarm. The hunters have missed this time, but they will not go hungry. There are plenty more birds—as well as fish and bigger game such as deer—near their village of simple wooden huts.

Hunters have been wandering along the Thames riverbanks for as many as 200,000 years, but these Neolithic (New Stone Age) people are among the first to stop and clear the woodland. In addition to hunting and collecting plant foods, like their ancestors before them, they have also begun to grow crops and herd animals in the spaces they have cleared.

They have built their village on a high gravel bank. It has good soil and is better drained than the surrounding marsh. It stays dry even when the river floods. The water here is shallow and easy to cross. In the future these benefits will attract more and more families to the spot. Some will settle here for good, marking the beginning of the place we now call "London."

wolves prowl in the dense undergrowth

the shallow River Thames winds slowly through reedy islands and sandbanks

The Neolithic people are creating and decorating clay pots and shaping flint chips into razor-sharp tools.

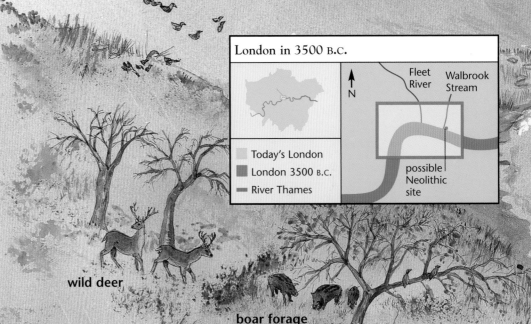

London in 3500 B.C.

Fleet River

Walbrook Stream

N

Today's London
London 3500 B.C.
River Thames

possible Neolithic site

wild deer

boar forage for food

woodland covers all
of the higher land

burning trees and
bushes clears land
for settlement

Houses built from poles and mud
and roofed with straw thatch
are simple but warm and dry.

the roofs are thatched
with reeds or leaves

the huts have
wooden frames

this stream is
now known as
Walbrook Stream

a muddy mixture
(daub) covers walls
woven with sticks (wattles)

sheep are raised for milk
and wool, but not meat

the high riverbank
keeps the settlement
above free from floods

everyone knows
how to make useful
tools from stone

wild ducks

fish from the river
will be grilled over hot
embers from the fire

some Neolithic people still
lead the same nomadic
(wandering) lives as their
ancestors did

hunters have
tamed dogs to
help them catch
animals for food

animal skins
provide clothes
for everyone

woven wooden
walkways cross
marshland and
shallow water

The riverbank people are religious.
They have marked their sacred path
with a cursus—a pair of ditches.

another Roman camp lies to the south, over the horizon

the Roman plank bridge, or pontoon, rests on boat hulls

an advancing group of Roman soldiers sneaks up on the village

the boats are anchored to sunken, rock-filled baskets

fences stop animals from eating the food crops

the central wooden temple is supported by large wooden posts driven into the ground

wheat grows in small fields

Roman invasion

A.D. 43

Black crows rise from the trees as a distant trumpet blast shatters the morning calm. The sound brings everyone in the riverside village running from their round huts. The Celtic people, who now live on the riverbank, are under attack by the Romans! Their wooden fence keeps out curious animals, but it provides little protection against the mightiest army in the world.

the Celtic settlers have cleared more land for farming

The Romans, a people from the warm Mediterranean, have already conquered most of Europe. Their soldiers are highly trained and well equipped. A fine road network allows them to march quickly from their Italian homeland to patrol their empire. Now they have reached Britain. A terrifying armored elephant leads 40,000 soldiers over the floating bridge they have constructed across the river.

the Celtic warriors are ill-equipped to face the Roman threat

a high wall of wooden stakes protects the village

a temporary Roman camp

the Roman soldiers have pitched their leather tents

the "war elephant" is a Roman weapon of terror

soldiers wait to cross the river

The villagers know how to defend themselves. They have iron swords and helmets. Other Celtic tribes to the southeast of this settlement held back the Roman army for two whole days. The women grab their children and their most valuable possessions, then flee. The warriors who remain soon realize they cannot win. They surrender without a fight. Over the next few years the Romans will conquer all of England and Wales.

villagers flee with whatever they can carry

The Romans bring elephants to battle to frighten enemies who may not have seen the animals before.

pottery and fine metal vessels are precious possessions

In ceremonies to honor water gods, priests toss valuable metal objects into the River Thames.

animals now graze on vegetation in the cursus ditches

pigs feast on fallen acorns

London in A.D. 43

N

Fleet River

Walbrook Stream

Today's London

London A.D. 43

River Thames

possible Celtic site

Boudicca attacks!

A.D. 60

Under Roman control, solid houses replace the Celtic huts on the riverbank. By A.D. 60 the small town is a center for trading on land and water. A stone forum (market building) stands on a main road. Ships from France and Italy sail up the Thames to unload wine at the quayside next to a sturdy bridge. The Romans of "Londinium" feel safe. They have not even built a wall to defend their town.

They pay a high price for their overconfidence. The Iceni, a tribe of Celtic people from eastern England, have rebelled. Romans have whipped their queen, Boudicca, and abused her daughters. Now the Iceni people want revenge. Their warriors advance to Londinium. Terrified of what is to come, the city's governor, Suetonius, orders his people to flee.

Boudicca (died c. A.D. 60) roars, "Let's show the Romans they are hares trying to rule over wolves."

even those who hide cannot escape the vengeful Iceni

Commander Gaius Suetonius Paulinus directs the Roman retreat

Romans flee across a wooden bridge that spans the River Thames

traders' houses near the wharf burn

Iceni rebels search for valuables to loot

ships have been set on fire

flaming sails threaten to burn other ships in the harbor

sailors try to flee on ships moored at the quayside

London in A.D. 60

Today's London
London A.D. 60
River Thames

Fleet River
Walbrook Stream
N

there are no walls or ditches to defend the city from attack

Iceni warriors attack the Roman stragglers as they attempt to flee Londinium on foot.

a network of well-built roads makes escape easy and quick

Iceni warriors push a burning hay wagon down a hill, toward Roman buildings

most residents fled hours earlier, leaving streets empty

Iceni warriors set buildings on fire

the forum (market building) is the only solid stone building in the settlement

captured Romans face horrible deaths

Queen Boudicca riding on her chariot

wood-and-thatch houses burn fiercely

The streets are almost empty when the Celtic army attacks. They take their revenge ruthlessly. They torture and kill any Romans they find and steal anything of value. Finally, they set the town on fire. However, Roman troops stationed in Londinium have escaped. They soon retaliate against the rebellious Britons. Defeated, Boudicca poisons herself, and the Romans return to rebuild their shattered town.

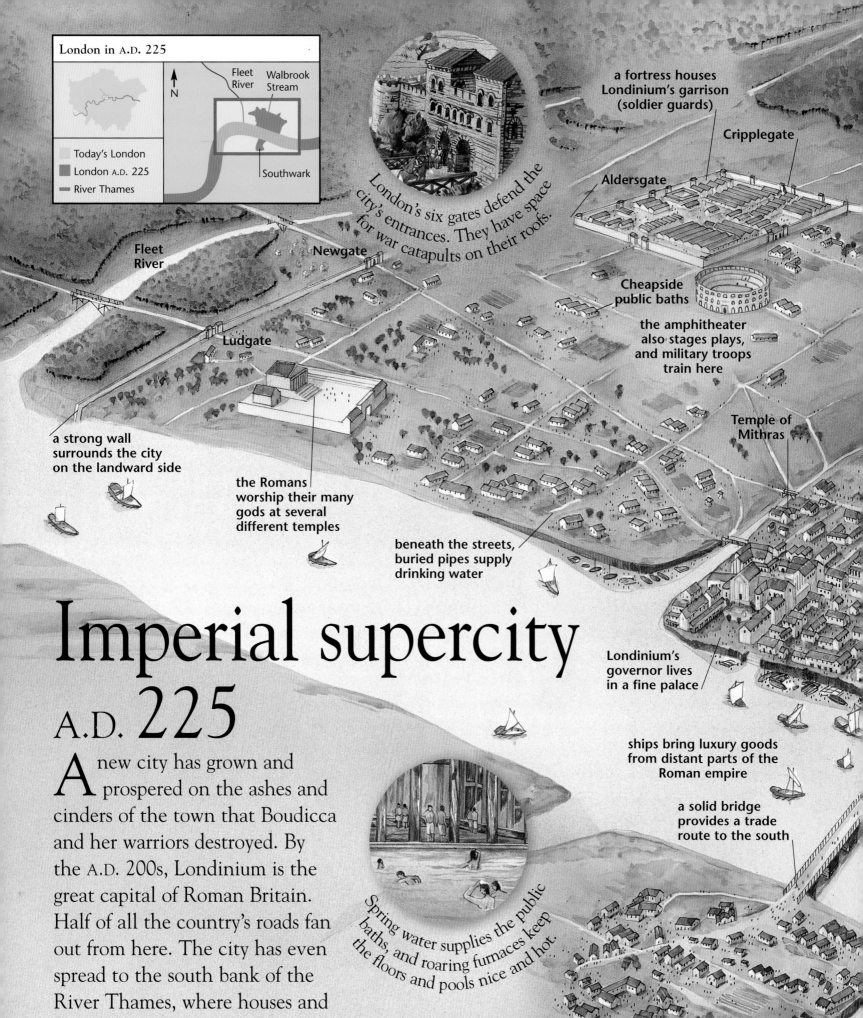

Today's London
London A.D. 225
River Thames

N

Fleet River
Walbrook Stream

Southwark

London's six gates defend the city's entrances. They have space for war catapults on their roofs.

a fortress houses Londinium's garrison (soldier guards)

Cripplegate

Aldersgate

Fleet River

Newgate

Cheapside public baths

the amphitheater also stages plays, and military troops train here

Ludgate

Temple of Mithras

a strong wall surrounds the city on the landward side

the Romans worship their many gods at several different temples

beneath the streets, buried pipes supply drinking water

Londinium's governor lives in a fine palace

Imperial supercity

A.D. 225

A new city has grown and prospered on the ashes and cinders of the town that Boudicca and her warriors destroyed. By the A.D. 200s, Londinium is the great capital of Roman Britain. Half of all the country's roads fan out from here. The city has even spread to the south bank of the River Thames, where houses and shops cluster around the end of the timber bridge.

ships bring luxury goods from distant parts of the Roman empire

a solid bridge provides a trade route to the south

Spring water supplies the public baths, and roaring furnaces keep the floors and pools nice and hot.

the bridge has allowed Londinium to spread to the south bank of the river

beyond the city, the Thames valley is still heavily forested

Walbrook Stream

Londinium's wealthy people have made their city as much like Rome as possible. They wash, swim, and sweat in two public baths. They worship their many gods in the city's temples. There are fashionable shops and heated homes. Government offices line an impressive basilica. There is even a round amphitheater (stadium) where up to 9,000 spectators can watch gladiators fight to the death.

stone for the city wall comes by river from quarries about 45 mi. (75km) away

Roman roads will set the city's layout until the present day

Bishopsgate

the basilica provides space for shops and offices

cemetery

Aldgate

forum

the roads, stretching in all directions, are now paved in stone

The Romans have learned a valuable lesson from Boudicca's victory. To protect Londinium from attack there is now a high wall with 40 towers and strong gate houses. Soldiers from the city's fortress patrol it day and night. The wall, and the roads that divide up the city, will outlive Roman rule. Eighteen centuries into the future, they will continue to shape the city's outline.

bustling wharf area with trading ships

a higher sea level means tides now swell the River Thames twice daily

the Romans will eventually continue the city wall along the river to protect against an attack from the water

A Mithraeum temple reminds worshipers of the cave where the god Mithras killed a sacred bull.

A Viking raid
A.D. 851

T he rising tide washes them up the Thames—a huge fleet of ships with tall, terrifying warriors at the oars. The Vikings run ashore and attack like hungry wolves. These men are Danish pirates. Their repeated raids threaten the very survival of this small riverside town and its Saxon people.

the Roman city wall

the Saxon houses are low, simple shelters

valuable livestock are herded away to the safety of fields to the north

the Saxon settlement is on the site of present-day London's famous Covent Garden market

the riverside marketplace is already a center for international trade

the tall Viking warriors are terrifying figures

as they leave, the Vikings start fires that will burn Lundenwic to the ground

the Lundenwic "docks" are little more than plank jetties

the Vikings carry off the healthy, young, and beautiful to sell as slaves

Four centuries earlier, the Saxons came from Germany, taking over the region as Roman power weakened. They settled west of Londinium, building a riverside hamlet, named Lundenwic, and farming the land around it. A Christian people, they have built churches near the river. The Viking invaders head for these buildings first. They know they will find rich booty in these sacred places.

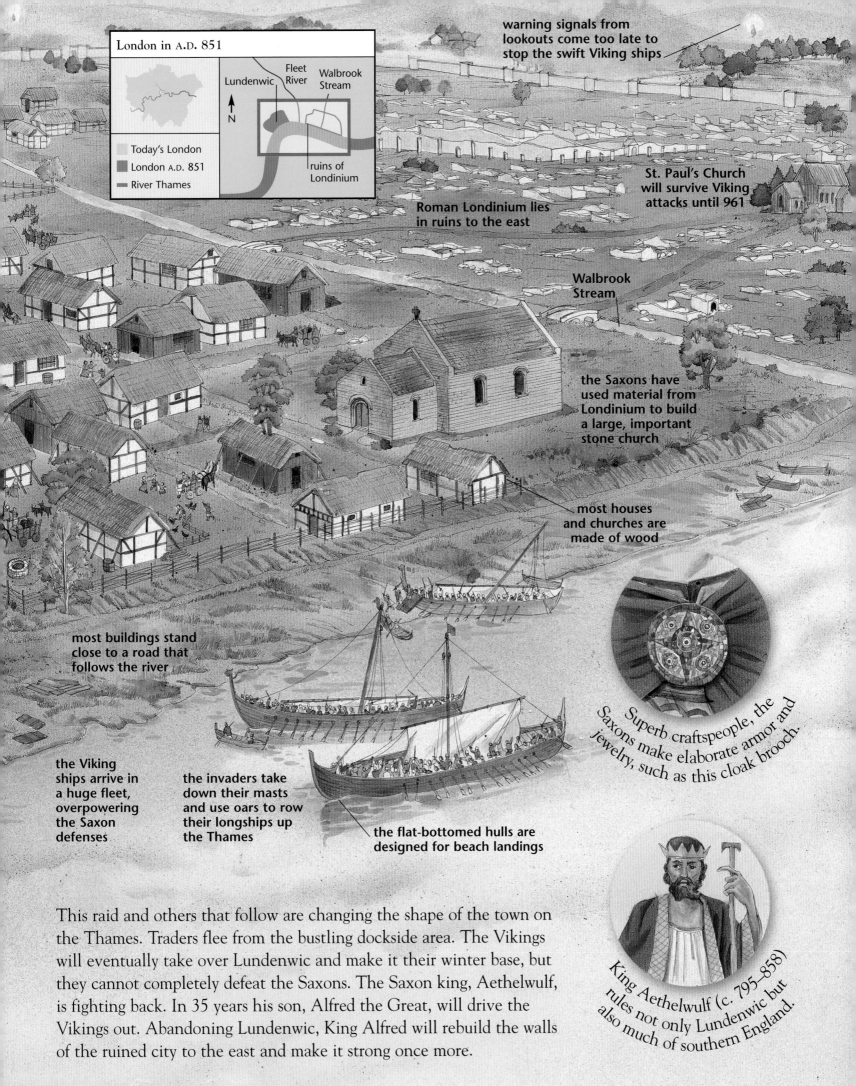

London in A.D. 851

Lundenwic   Fleet River   Walbrook Stream

N

ruins of Londinium

Today's London
London A.D. 851
River Thames

warning signals from lookouts come too late to stop the swift Viking ships

Roman Londinium lies in ruins to the east

St. Paul's Church will survive Viking attacks until 961

Walbrook Stream

the Saxons have used material from Londinium to build a large, important stone church

most houses and churches are made of wood

most buildings stand close to a road that follows the river

the Viking ships arrive in a huge fleet, overpowering the Saxon defenses

the invaders take down their masts and use oars to row their longships up the Thames

the flat-bottomed hulls are designed for beach landings

Superb craftspeople, the Saxons make elaborate armor and jewelry, such as this cloak brooch.

This raid and others that follow are changing the shape of the town on the Thames. Traders flee from the bustling dockside area. The Vikings will eventually take over Lundenwic and make it their winter base, but they cannot completely defeat the Saxons. The Saxon king, Aethelwulf, is fighting back. In 35 years his son, Alfred the Great, will drive the Vikings out. Abandoning Lundenwic, King Alfred will rebuild the walls of the ruined city to the east and make it strong once more.

King Aethelwulf (c. 795–858) rules not only Lundenwic but also much of southern England.

15

one platform
lifts to let large
ships pass through

a wooden
bridge crosses
the Thames

most houses still
have wooden frames
and thatched roofs

strong winds have
torn down part of the
tower and flattened
600 houses

Norman London

A.D. 1091

local stonemasons
and laborers are
forced to work
on the fortress

In London's eastern corner, masons are toiling on a huge, tall castle. Once again London has new foreign rulers. William of Normandy, France, invaded England twenty-five years ago, in 1066. Renamed William the Conqueror, the French king strengthened his grip over England's fierce and restless people. The White Tower is simply the grandest among a chain of strongholds that the Normans have constructed.

the Normans
transport stone
from quarries
in France

William made London the capital of England, so he had to bring the city completely under his control. To the west, just outside the city walls, Westminster is now a center for the law and the site of a royal palace. Inside the walls, merchants handle local and international trade. London is a religious center, too, with many new churches and monasteries under construction.

A powerful gale rips through London in 1091, tearing off church roofs and damaging the bridge.

wooden posts have
been used to turn
muddy riverbanks
into solid wharves
(piers)

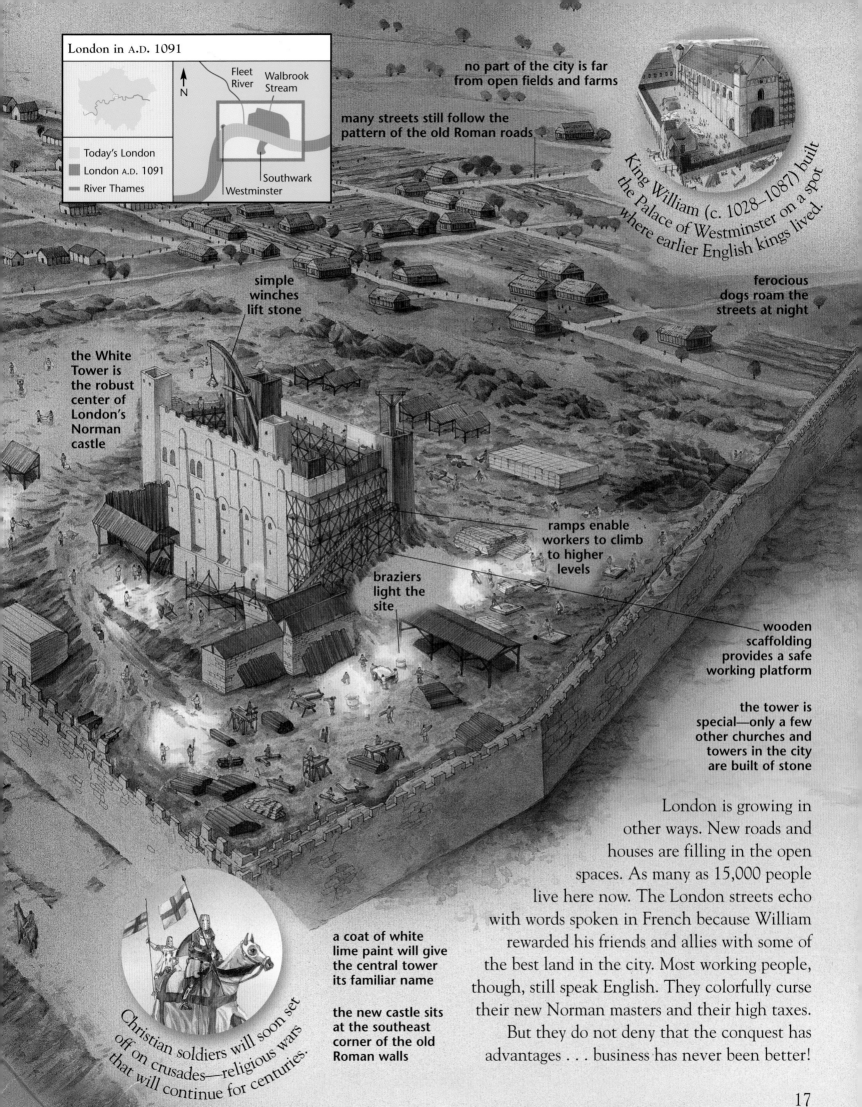

London in A.D. 1091

Fleet River
Walbrook Stream
N
Southwark
Westminster

Today's London
London A.D. 1091
River Thames

no part of the city is far from open fields and farms

many streets still follow the pattern of the old Roman roads

King William (c. 1028–1087) built the Palace of Westminster on a spot where earlier English kings lived.

ferocious dogs roam the streets at night

simple winches lift stone

the White Tower is the robust center of London's Norman castle

ramps enable workers to climb to higher levels

braziers light the site

wooden scaffolding provides a safe working platform

the tower is special—only a few other churches and towers in the city are built of stone

a coat of white lime paint will give the central tower its familiar name

the new castle sits at the southeast corner of the old Roman walls

Christian soldiers will soon set off on crusades—religious wars that will continue for centuries.

London is growing in other ways. New roads and houses are filling in the open spaces. As many as 15,000 people live here now. The London streets echo with words spoken in French because William rewarded his friends and allies with some of the best land in the city. Most working people, though, still speak English. They colorfully curse their new Norman masters and their high taxes. But they do not deny that the conquest has advantages . . . business has never been better!

Bridge of stone
A.D. 1216

Since ancient times, Londoners have crossed the swirling, salty waters of the River Thames on wooden bridges. Wars, fires, floods, ice, gales, and rot have destroyed them one after another. Then, in the 1100s, priest and bridgemaster Peter de Colechurch decided it was time for something stronger and sturdier: a bridge made of stone.

London's new bridge was completed seven years ago, in 1209. Today, in the summer of 1216, it is at the center of a political revolution. England's unpopular King John (1167–1216) is at war with his powerful barons. Weary of his hopeless leadership, they have invited the French king, Louis VIII (1187–1226), to take John's place as ruler. Louis and his knights pause briefly at the bridge gates before crossing amid cheering crowds.

London's fine cathedral, St. Paul's, will host the French king's welcome ceremony

colors from the bankside dye works tint the water

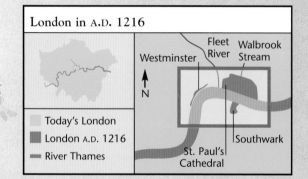

London in A.D. 1216

Today's London
London A.D. 1216
River Thames

Westminster
Fleet River
Walbrook Stream
N
St. Paul's Cathedral
Southwark

during Roman times, London began spreading out around the south end of the bridge

the neighborhood on this side of the bridge is called Southwark, meaning "southern fortress"

ferrymen take passengers across the Thames

most London houses are still built out of wood

house of the Bishop of Winchester

Southwark is built on what was once marshland

Soon after his arrival, Louis is declared king at a special ceremony inside St. Paul's.

Southwark Priory

before the arrival of the French, the English king, John, fled across the bridge to Winchester

fireproof stone and tiled
roofs are gradually
replacing thatch

bridgemaster Peter de
Colechurch died before his
work was complete, and
his body was entombed
inside St. Thomas's chapel
on the bridge

two Roman roads meet
at the end of the bridge

houses and shops
cluster on either side
of the narrow
roadway

a noisy crowd
begins to gather
on the bridge

ships dock with
fish, wine, grain,
and cloth at
riverside wharves

a stone bridge
has replaced the
wooden river
crossing

London Bridge still has
one span (platform)
that opens to allow
larger boats through

London's first mayor,
Henry Fitz-Ailwyn,
greets the French
king at a stone
gateway at the
south end of
the bridge

Without the smell and sound of the
water below them, the visitors would
not know they were crossing a river.
Houses and shops line the roadway,
crowding in on them. Shopkeepers
shout from doorways. Residents
empty stinking chamber pots from
their windows. Beggars plead for
change, and thieves eye the fat purses
of the new arrivals. In fact, London
Bridge gives the French king a vivid
first glimpse of the noisy, smelly,
violent, bustling city beyond.

Louis VIII has ridden 60 mi.
(100km) from the English coast

French knights carry the
king's gold-and-blue
royal emblem

One year ago, the barons forced
King John to sign the Magna Carta
and agree to the laws set out in it.

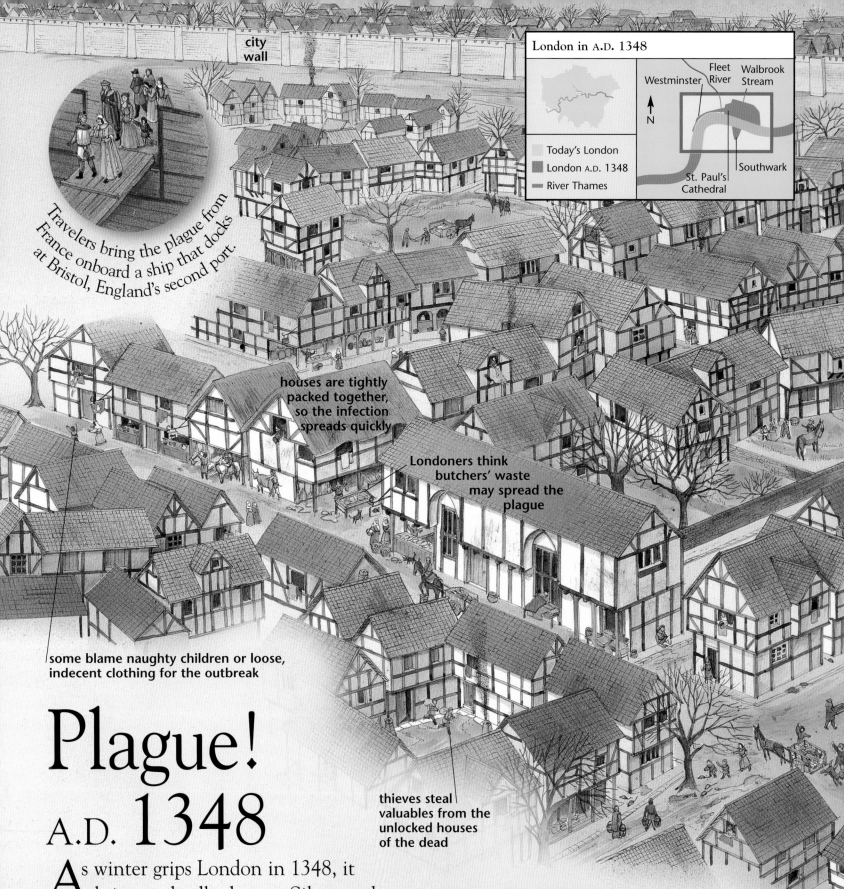

city wall

Travelers bring the plague from France onboard a ship that docks at Bristol, England's second port.

London in A.D. 1348

Today's London
London A.D. 1348
River Thames

Westminster
Fleet River
Walbrook Stream
St. Paul's Cathedral
Southwark
N

houses are tightly packed together, so the infection spreads quickly

Londoners think butchers' waste may spread the plague

some blame naughty children or loose, indecent clothing for the outbreak

Plague!
A.D. 1348

thieves steal valuables from the unlocked houses of the dead

As winter grips London in 1348, it brings a deadly danger. Silent and invisible, a killer stalks the empty streets. Terrified citizens have heard rumors of the threat and stay indoors, but this does not save them. One-fourth of London's people die. Their killer is the plague, the most deadly disease ever to strike the city.

Nicknamed the "Black Death," after the dark color it turns the skin, the sickness spreads quickly. Worn down by cold, wet weather, and hunger, the city folk have little strength left to fight the illness. When they catch it, apple-sized swellings appear in their groin or armpits. They cough up blood and die within days. Doctors' "cures," such as draining the blood, only make the plague sufferers die faster.

so many have died that some streets are now empty

the poor are buried by the dozen in huge pits outside the city walls

The plague kills young and old, rich and poor without mercy. Some who can afford to flee survive—but their escape helps spread the disease beyond London. The worst hit are those in crowded, stinking slums. At first families bury their dead in local churchyards, but as the bodies pile up Londoners dig large pits to serve as mass graves. The plague ends in the spring, but there will be four more epidemics before the end of the century.

Three cold, wet summers in a row have ruined the harvests, so many Londoners are almost starving.

wealthy people flee and spread the plague elsewhere

corpse carriers take dead bodies to mass burial sites

cold, wet weather means people are weak and hungry

In the plague pits of East Smithfield, as many as 200 victims share each huge grave.

the city has no sewage system—diseases breed in the filthy streets

only the wealthy get individual graves

space for graves will soon run out in the churchyards

even the poorest citizens are given a proper Christian burial

religious people flog themselves to beg for God's mercy

fleas on black rats may be spreading the plague

hungry dogs run amok

medical "cures" do not work

21

The age of print
A.D. 1476

At the back of a shop in the shadow of Westminster Abbey, a worker heaves on a lever, and inky metal letters squeeze against wet paper. Peeling off the page, he hangs it up to dry with many other printed sheets. Bound into books, the pages he is printing are transforming London—and Britain. They are spreading knowledge faster and farther than ever before.

The owner of the workshop is William Caxton. A merchant and writer, he learned the secret of printing in Germany, where it was invented 40 years ago. Before then books were rare and very expensive because priests and monks had to write every word by hand. Caxton's presses can print 1,000 books in the time it takes to copy one with a pen.

Westminster is green with meadows and farmland—and farm animals are still a common sight

the monks of nearby Westminster Abbey give money to support the Almonry residents

Westminster Abbey

the gardens are planted with herbs and divided up with crisscrossed paths

printed books have made learning easier for boys at Westminster and other schools

a wooden press squeezes paper onto the inked type

Caxton's workshop is in the Almonry—a courtyard of shops and houses for the poor

drying sheets of printed paper

the typesetter arranges tiny lead letters, called "type," into words and sentences

the printer dabs ink onto the metal type using leather pads

herb clippings, known as "strew," are thrown onto indoor floors to sweeten the stale air

William Caxton (c. 1415–1492) is the first to print books in the English language.

London in A.D. 1476

Westminster
St. Paul's Cathedral
N
Tower of London
Southwark

Today's London
London A.D. 1476
River Thames

Westminster is royal London: King Edward IV (1442–1483) has his palace close to Caxton's shop.

scribes copying books by hand fear they will lose their jobs because of the new printing press

the Palace of Westminster, by the river, is the king's London home

Westminster Hall

the City of London lies about 1.2 mi. (2km) to the east

St. Paul's Cathedral

the King's Bridge

Royal Chancery

Organized in guilds, London's traders and craftworkers keep tight control of the city's businesses.

a gardener is clipping the hedges to gather "strew"

Thames lightermen (barge operators) bring paper from London's docks farther downriver

by following every path, visitors can exercise in a small area

The printing press makes book production cheaper, so more people than ever are learning to read. Printing enables scientists to tell people about what they learn, leading to a revolution in discovery and invention. By taking bookmaking out of the churches and monasteries, printing will also help spread new ideas about religion.

Caxton imports his paper from France and Italy

the River Thames is the city's main route of transportation

dumped rubbish and sewage block the smelly Fleet River

Baynard's Castle is a royal palace: the keeper entertained the queen with a banquet and firework display here

many of the theaters cluster on the south bank of the river, outside the control of the city council

William Shakespeare (1564–1616) writes 38 plays in all and becomes the world's most famous playwright.

ferrymen bring theater-goers across the river

the Rose was the first theater to be built on Bankside, in 1586–1587

the Globe and Rose theaters often compete with each other for audiences

Shakespeare belongs to a theater company called the Lord Chamberlain's Men

Rose theater

street vendor

to stand in the theater costs one penny; to sit costs two; and for three pence spectators get a seat with a cushion

doughnut-shaped playhouse gives all a good view

Globe theater

the roof over the stage keeps the rain and sun off the costumes, some costing £15,000 ($22,000) in today's money

young male actors play all the female parts

building materials for the theaters came from another dismantled theater in north London

Shakespeare is also part owner of the Globe theater

standing spectators are known as "groundlings" or "stinkards"

hazelnut shells keep the ground from getting muddy when it rains

Shakespeare's London

A.D. 1602

As the actors appear on the stage, the chattering crowd falls silent. They have dragged themselves across the river to see a play, paying twice the normal price. It is the first public performance of *Twelfth Night*, and they want to hear every word. Beside the stage, the playwright, William Shakespeare, smiles with satisfaction: another full house . . .

monks from an abbey in Surrey stay at Chertsey House when they visit London

Formed last year in a London pub, the East India Company will first trade with India and then rule it.

Broken Wharf got its name because it crumbled while its two owners argued for 40 years over the cost of repairs

St. Mary Overie's Dock

Bankside's entertainment includes bearbaiting pits, where chained bears are forced to fight with hunting dogs

English people will look back on Elizabeth I's reign (1558–1603) as a "golden age" of prosperity and culture.

people watch their step in these streets because there are no restrooms in the theaters

Shakespeare's company has built a theater, the Globe, at Bankside. This is a rough area of drunkenness and crime—but it is beyond the control of London's councilors, who say actors are no better than tramps who spread disease, noise, and disorder. But Elizabeth I disagrees. Though old and tired after more than 40 years as queen, she loves the theater and gives support to Shakespeare's company.

Others are also benefitting from the queen's interest. Her long reign has made London more wealthy. Ships from the Thames have defeated an invading Spanish fleet. City merchants have set up one of Europe's first stock exchanges. Their expeditions have explored the world, bringing riches back to London. Sitting in the Globe theater's best seats, these wealthy traders will applaud wildly at the end of the play.

London in A.D. 1602

Westminster
St. Paul's Cathedral
N
Today's London
London A.D. 1602
River Thames
Baynard's Castle
Southwark

London in A.D. 1666

Westminster
Tower of London
N
Today's London
London A.D. 1666
River Thames
St. Paul's Cathedral
Southwark

London Bridge

firefighters tear down houses to keep the flames from spreading

Pudding Lane

landlords try to protect their houses from demolition—until they feel the fierce heat of the blaze

sparks light the straw in the yard of the Star Inn

frightened dogs run amok

pumps on wheels or sleds shoot water at the burning buildings

one rich Londoner throws a hatful of money into the crowd to encourage people to fight the flames

there are water barrels in the streets for use in case of fires, but they are useless against such a huge blaze—and they soon run dry

people drag their belongings to the river, hoping to save them in a boat

26

The Great Fire
A.D. 1666

Southwark

the fire melts the bells in city churches

stray sparks ignite the dry thatch roofs

the streets are so narrow that flames can lick straight across them—and spread the fire

the baker and his family escape across the roofs

upper floors are built outward, narrowing the streets further

scared of heights, the baker's maid stays behind—and burns

the wooden buildings burn quickly

the weatherproof coat of pitch on the bakery walls easily catches on fire

sailors blow up houses to create firebreaks, which will keep the flames from spreading

the fire started at Thomas Farriner's bakery in Pudding Lane

Hot and crackling, yellow tongues of flame lick from the windows of a bakery on Pudding Lane. Just after midnight on September 2, a tiny spark from the oven has lit bundles of dry twigs stacked nearby. Within an hour the blaze spreads to the whole of the street. Then the flames ignite nearby warehouses storing oil, spirits, and pitch.

At first few Londoners worry. Fires are common. Even the mayor is not concerned: he takes a good look at the fire and goes back to bed, thinking it is not a problem. He is wrong. A strong wind fans the flames. Buckets of water, the only common fire precaution, cannot quench them. When the fire reaches London Bridge, it burns the water wheels that pump vital river water all over the city.

Writer Samuel Pepys (1633–1703) describes the fire in his diary: to save his best cheese, he buries it.

Ferrymen helping families escape across the river make a healthy profit by doubling their fares.

As soon as it is clear their city is doomed, Londoners begin to flee. Taking only what they can carry, they escape across the river on a fleet of boats. Just six people die. From the south bank, they watch for three days as a circle of flame eats up nine-tenths of their homes and possessions. But even before the ashes are cold, London's leaders are planning a new city.

From the ashes
A.D. 1707

The destruction of London more than 40 years ago was not all bad news. The flames swept away crowded, filthy, and unhealthy streets. In their place Londoners built a new, finer city. Inns and houses were first to be built to new safety codes, using fireproof materials. They lined most of the burned streets just six years after the fire.

Public buildings were more difficult. Officials turned down several designs for a grand grid of new avenues. Instead they sketched in the city hall, stock exchange, customhouse, and merchants' halls on roads that followed ancient routes. A tax on coal paid for the rebuilding work. To replace more than 50 churches lost in the flames, they called on the gifted scientist and architect Christopher Wren.

Christopher Wren (1632–1723) shared his work on the churches with several other architects.

This huge task has taken up half of Wren's life, but now it is almost complete. The last church to be finished is the biggest: St. Paul's. To watch masons and carpenters working at dizzying heights, Wren is hoisted to the top in a basket. He is eager to check the details of the cathedral's crown—an immense dome. With a gray lead skin, it will become one of London's—and Britain's—most famous landmarks.

all roofing materials are now fireproof

wooden structures are forbidden—walls are now brick or stone

the streets are now wider, but most still trace the pattern they followed before the fire

the old, ruined cathedral was demolished using controlled explosions, which locals mistook for earthquakes

the center-line of the cathedral lines up exactly with the rising sun on Easter morning

tired of people interfering, Wren hides the construction site behind huge wattle screens

wooden crane

the stones had to be winched up a hill from the river—the largest took one week to move

the cathedral costs a fortune to construct

workers are paid not by the hour, but by the foot of work completed

work on St. Paul's Cathedral, the largest burned building, began after most of the other buildings were complete

the site is guarded by watchmen and two large mastiff dogs

28

just months before the Great Fire, Wren had suggested adding a dome to the old St. Paul's

a cross is being erected at the top, 364 ft. (111m) above the ground

Wren alters the details of the cathedral and its dome while work is in progress

The finished cathedral is very different from the plans that Wren drew up to get his designs approved.

a wooden frame supports the outer dome

a supporting cone is made of brick

the smaller, inner dome is the cathedral ceiling

two huge iron chains ring the twin domes to stop their bases from spreading

lead outer skin

In the 1680s and 1690s, the winters were often cold enough to hold fairs on the frozen Thames.

a whisper inside the gallery can be heard clearly on the other side, 108 ft. (33m) away

London in A.D. 1707

Westminster Abbey

Tower of London

N

Today's London

London A.D. 1707

River Thames

St. Paul's Cathedral

Southwark

at the peak of construction, 400 men are at work on the site

workers digging foundations for new buildings unearth thick charcoal—a residue of wood burned in the Great Fire

Georgian London

A.D. 1783

England's King George III (1738–1820) rules his realm from a divided city. It is not a high wall that cuts London in half, but money and class. Wealthy, noble Londoners live luxuriously in the grand new houses that are springing up everywhere. Yet in the mean streets nearby, children roam in packs and have to steal in order to eat.

Businessmen meet in London's coffeehouses (cafés) to exchange news and gossip and to make deals.

drovers herd geese from Wales to the London markets

elegant houses, but no stores, line fashionable Oxford Street

a highwayman is being driven to the gallows in Tyburn—to be hanged

huge crowds follow the cart to watch the execution

Hangings in Tyburn are like festivals: people take the day off to watch criminals die.

rich Londoners take carriages to their gambling clubs

London's worst slums cluster around the church of St. Giles. It is in this neighborhood that the two sides of London come face to face. Of every ten children born here, only one will live to age five—and will probably survive by picking the pockets of the wealthy. If caught, that child will die on the gallows (by hanging). At this time, brutal laws punish even minor crimes with execution.

wealthy people risk being robbed in broad daylight

wealthy noblemen own whole blocks of fine homes—the best look out across leafy Bedford Square

merchants, having grown rich from trade, live in many of the grand houses

Yet only a few hundred yards away lies a beautiful leafy square. The elegant houses around it are the homes of some of London's richest families. The wealthy owners would not risk walking through the nearby streets, so carriages take them to their private clubs. There they drink, dine, and gamble away the fortunes they have made— perhaps by trading African slaves for Jamaican sugar.

London in A.D. 1783

Westminster Abbey
Tower of London

N

Today's London
London A.D. 1783
River Thames

St. Paul's Cathedral
Southwark

coffeehouses are popular meeting places—for those who can afford coffee

craftworkers, such as knife sharpeners, labor in small, cramped rooms

St. Giles Circus, a crossroads, is named after a nearby church

the slum area is nicknamed a "rookery," after the birds' noisy, crowded nests

men condemned to be hanged often have one last drink at the Angel Inn

one house in every four sells cheap gin (an alcoholic drink)

there are drunks on every street

street hawkers sell oranges, onions, herring, and watercress

a thief

badly built slum houses often collapse

several families may share one room

St. Giles church

31

The Great Exhibition
A.D. 1851

Glittering like a diamond in London's biggest park, "Crystal Palace" looks like a gigantic greenhouse. Though there are some plants—and even trees—inside, the crowds flocking through the doors swiftly pass these by. For this magnificent structure has been built to house an extraordinary exhibition, showing off the arts and industries of Great Britain and the rest of the world.

Architect Joseph Paxton (1803–1865) modeled Crystal Palace on a water-lily greenhouse.

the River Thames snakes off to the southeast

the design of Crystal Palace is based on a greenhouse

the top panes of glass are as high as an eight-story building

standard-size parts were used in the construction to speed up the building work

the giant glass building is big enough to enclose whole elm trees

at 1,850 ft. (564m), the building is longer than five football fields

even with 93,000 people inside, the halls never seem crowded

laid flat, the glass panes would cover about 320 tennis courts

the visitors number six million in total— about one-third of Great Britain's population

entry to the exhibition costs one shilling—one-third of a laborer's daily wage

a London omnibus

Suggested by Prince Albert, the husband of Queen Victoria (1819–1901), the Exhibition is a spectacular success. Every major nation has sent exhibits. Visitors gasp at the giant steam-powered machines. They wonder at marvels such as a piano for four players, and they laugh at sculptures made out of soap. One-third of Great Britain's people visit: their tickets not only pay for the show but also provide enough extra money to build three new museums nearby.

Crystal Palace itself is as much a source of wonder as what is inside. It has been built in only nine months, using a castiron frame and glass sheets. When the show ends, it will be taken down, moved 7.5 mi. (12km) and reconstructed. A source of great pride for Londoners, the building and exhibition seem to sum up their city and country: wealthy, grand, proud, and powerful.

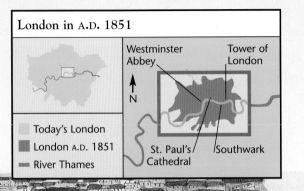

London in A.D. 1851

Westminster Abbey

Tower of London

N

Today's London
London A.D. 1851
River Thames

St. Paul's Cathedral

Southwark

A display of moving machinery demonstrates how to save on human labor in industry.

The queen opens the show twice: once in Hyde Park and again when it is moved to south London.

profits from the exhibition will pay for new museums in nearby South Kensington

14,000 different exhibitors are putting their goods on display

even the world's largest diamond, called the Koh-i-Noor, is on show inside Crystal Palace

the American exhibit, the biggest in the show, includes a huge piano—for up to four pianists—and sculptures made out of soap

most of the machines on show are steam powered—engineers refer to electric machines as "toys"

visitors are excited by the gigantic size of the exhibition

Strand Bridge, or Waterloo Bridge

shipbuilders and timber yards rely on the river for trade and deliveries

electricity powers the modern flour mills

molten lead, poured from the tall shot tower, forms tiny pellets for shotguns

carts pulled by huge horses deliver beer from a brewery

the Embankment (riverside) area was one of the first places in Great Britain to have electric streetlights

a railroad bridge crosses the River Thames to Charing Cross Station

trains from Waterloo Station connect the capital to south and southwest England

London is home to the world's first underground railway. More are being built to reduce road traffic.

a "funeral train" takes coffins to a cemetery outside London

horses still pull even the biggest vehicles

the chimneys of glass and pottery kilns (ovens) belch out dark smoke, which blackens other buildings

small workshops make clothes, furniture, silk, hats, jewelry, and guns

London's streets are choked with heavy traffic

St. John's church

many streets are still lit by gas lamps

Industrial giant
A.D. 1900

In the year 1900, London is the world's biggest city. At its bustling center, workshops and mills mingle with rows of houses for their workers. Every day, the trains bring thousands more. Among the horse-drawn traffic that chokes the streets is a new sight—the automobile. Electricity is replacing steam and gas, powering streetlights and underground trains.

The roads around London's biggest train station seem to be thriving. Riverside factories make a vast range of products—boats, glass, pottery, beer, jam, vinegar, and furniture—for sale in Britain and abroad. Though grimed with soot, the houses are better than the slums they replaced. New water and sewage programs have made the city a healthier place. Wages for London workers are rising steadily.

streets of houses cluster tightly around factories and warehouses

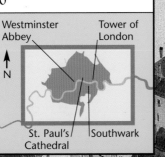

Until 1896, laws required a man with a red flag to walk in front of "horseless carriages" as a speed limit.

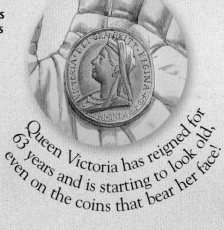

Queen Victoria has reigned for 63 years and is starting to look old, even on the coins that bear her face!

But Britain's "golden age" of world power is gone. Its capital's prosperity is fragile. The train station, Waterloo, is named after an 1815 battlefield victory that is proudly remembered but hard to repeat. London's industrial power is slipping, too. Fewer and fewer countries want their goods made in these factories. Soon the city and the nation will be struggling with bigger, better competitors—and enemies—overseas.

London in A.D. 1900

Westminster Abbey
Tower of London
N
St. Paul's Cathedral
Southwark

Today's London
London A.D. 1900
River Thames

Antiaircraft guns rarely hit the bombers—until computerized aiming arrives later in the war.

Deep underground railway tunnels are the only places that Londoners can sleep soundly during the bombings.

glowing "tracer" shells show the gunners where they are aiming

searchlight beams comfort Londoners but do not protect them from attacks

the bombs are not usually accurate enough to hit small targets such as a bridge or railroad track

Blackfriars Bridge

Waterloo Bridge

air-raid sirens at the top of tall pillars warn when bombers approach

antiaircraft guns

citizens file into underground air-raid shelters when the sirens sound

Hungerford Bridge

Waterloo Station

Families huddle in their backyards inside crude shelters made out of sheet steel and soil.

The Blitz
A.D. 1940

for each person the bombings kill, 35 more are made homeless

antiaircraft guns are set up all over London

St. Paul's Cathedral survives the bombings all around it

London's docks, to the east, are the main targets for the bombers

Southwark Bridge

the streets are unlit, to confuse the bomber pilots, and city cars have dimmed headlights

each citizen must carry a gas mask with him or her at all times

Londoners welcome American soldiers, whose help will enable Great Britain to defeat Germany.

sandbags protect doors from bomb blasts

German bombers are guided to target sites by radio beams, so they can attack what they cannot see.

Later in World War II (1939–1945), Germany will bombard London with crude rocket missiles called V-2s.

The moon rises over rain-swept London rooftops, sirens wail, and powerful searchlights crisscross the sky. The city is under attack! Great Britain is at war, and enemy aircraft are approaching with deadly cargoes of bombs. Clutching gas masks, Londoners scurry into underground shelters and jump at the sound of the first explosions, far to the east.

Londoners refer to the bombing as "the Blitz," taken from a German word, *Blitzkrieg*, which means "lightning war." They give it this name because the bombers are from Germany, Britain's enemy in the war. The Blitz began two months ago and has continued every night since. Though the bombers aim for the docks, many bombs miss their targets and instead fall on London homes. In the worst night of the Blitz, 1,400 people will die.

Londoners suffer because their city is almost defenseless. There are not enough public bomb shelters, searchlights are too weak, and the antiaircraft guns are too few. In the black sky, British fighter planes cannot find the bombers. But the government controls news reports to make it seem as if London is resisting and refusing to be beaten. Encouraged, the citizens get on with their lives—and, luckily for London, the Blitz fails.

London in A.D. 1940

Westminster Abbey

Tower of London

N

Today's London
London A.D. 1940
River Thames

St. Paul's Cathedral

Southwark

Fame and fashion
A.D. 1963

For a short time, in the 1960s, London is the capital of cool. Screaming music fans crowd into sold-out concerts. Everyone, everywhere, wants to wear clothes by London designers. Young Londoners lead a protest movement against war and against the old-fashioned attitudes of the past. Meanwhile, celebrity photographers capture the whole scene in gritty black-and-white images.

The streets themselves have not changed very much. New buildings fill the gaps left by wartime bombs, but the West End looks much as it did 50 years ago. Today a "ban the bomb" protest march fills the wide avenues. London's fashion center is nearby. Carnaby Street, in the seedy Soho neighborhood, is now home to trendy tailors and stores selling daring pop-art clothes.

in 1963 "ban the bomb" protests pave the way to an international treaty ending nuclear-weapons testing aboveground

the protesters block London's traffic

London's famous red "hop on, hop off" Routemaster buses will continue to carry passengers until 2005

this protest emblem has become an international symbol for peace

the demonstrators have marched from an atomic bomb factory in Aldermaston in southern England

London in A.D. 1963

Westminster Abbey
Tower of London
N
St. Paul's Cathedral
Southwark

Today's London
London A.D. 1963
River Thames

a tailor named John Stephen made Carnaby Street fashionable when he opened stores here

the slim, colorful look of London designer clothing will change fashions worldwide

men are wearing colorful clothing for the first time in centuries

trendy coffee shops line the streets of Soho

From Liverpool, in northern England, The Beatles are making British rock and pop music a success worldwide.

London is a center for new music, too. In a few months, a band called The Beatles will play at Soho's huge Palladium theater and establish itself as a global supergroup. Music pours from sweaty pubs, clubs, and coffee shops, too: jazz from Ronnie Scott's, rock 'n' roll from the Marquee and the 2i's coffee shop. Crowded with London's young, fashionable, well-dressed rebels, these cool venues make the city into one of the most happening places on the planet.

its international fame will soon turn Carnaby Street into a popular tourist attraction

Fashion designers are also setting up new boutiques on the exclusive King's Road in Chelsea, west London.

Groups of fashionable Londoners, known as "mods," wear trendy Italian suits and ride zippy Italian scooters.

homes, photographers' studios, galleries, and tailors' workshops fill the floors above Soho boutiques

fashionable mods flock to Soho's clubs to dance to popular ska and soul music

"tube" trains passing underground gently shake the sidewalks

mods ride Italian scooters

small, affordable cars are making driving much cheaper and more popular

London's streets were built for horses, so many are narrow for cars to use

at night, underground music swells from clubs in basements

39

Olympic city
Today

Neolithic people settled beside the River Thames because the high banks offered them safe homes and good hunting prospects. Today, London's City—as its financial district is known—is attractive for similar reasons. The residents are very different, though. Bankers and business tycoons have made this a place where great wealth can be earned—and lost. In towering glass offices, they hunt profits, not geese.

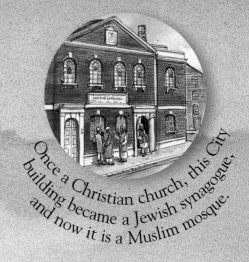

Once a Christian church, this City building became a Jewish synagogue, and now it is a Muslim mosque.

London in the present day

Westminster Abbey
Tower of London
N
Today's London
River Thames
St. Paul's Cathedral
Southwark

planners have preserved St. Paul's Cathedral and many other old City buildings

the "square mile" City is still London's main financial center

rising property prices have driven factories out of London's center

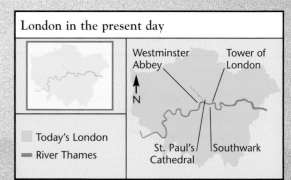

a replica of Shakespeare's Globe theater shows outdoor plays for today's public

many riverside wharf buildings are now expensive private apartments

this footbridge was nicknamed "the wobbly bridge" because it shook when it was first opened

the Millennium Bridge links St. Paul's Cathedral and the south bank

Tate Modern art gallery

the Thames is no longer a main transportation route, but it still carries leisure boats

Bankside Power Station, closed in 1981, is now one of the world's greatest modern art galleries

London now spreads out far beyond the City. Outside its ancient walls is a thriving modern capital. Centuries of trade, migration, and conquest have made it a place of many faces and races. Refugees took shelter here and then settled. They brought new art, language, food, and culture with them, making London an exciting, vibrant place to live and work.

A spectacular lightweight stadium will be the centerpiece of the 2012 Summer Olympic Games.

The curving roof of the Olympic Aquatics Centre mimics the shape of a breaking wave.

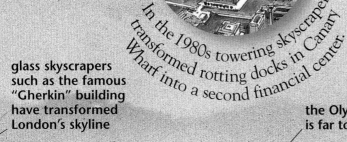

In the 1980s towering skyscrapers transformed rotting docks in Canary Wharf into a second financial center.

More change is on the way, too. On the horizon, tall cranes are building a new area, devoted to sports. In 2012, London will host the Summer Olympic Games. People of every nationality will come here to cheer on their athletes. And moving silently and unseen among them will be the spirits of the people who founded this great city thousands of years ago.

glass skyscrapers such as the famous "Gherkin" building have transformed London's skyline

the Olympic construction site is far to the east, in Stratford

London Bridge stands on the site of the ancient river crossing (see page 8)

Tower Bridge is named after the nearby castle—the Tower of London

Canary Wharf

London's modern government building is next to Tower Bridge

Southwark Bridge

Cannon Street railroad bridge

Glossary

Words in *italics* refer to other glossary entries.

Aethelwulf (c. 795–858)
A *Saxon* king of southern England who fought *Viking* raids on his lands.

Albert, Prince (1819–1861)
The husband of *Queen Victoria* who helped plan London's Great Exhibition of 1851.

amphitheater
A rounded stadium in which *Roman gladiators* fought to amuse spectators.

ancestor
Someone's parents, and also their grandparents, great-grandparents, and so on, through to the earliest members of a family.

Bankside
An area of the south bank of the River *Thames*, just west of *London Bridge*.

basilica
A building, usually found next to a *forum* in *Roman* cities, used for administration.

Black Death
A deadly *plague* that first struck Europe in the A.D. 1300s, killing up to half its population.

Blitz
A short form of *Blitzkrieg*, used to describe the German bombing of London in *World War II*.

Blitzkrieg
A German word meaning "lightning war."

Boudicca (or Boadicea, died c. A.D. 60)
The queen of the *Iceni* tribe who attacked and burned the Roman city of *Londinium* in A.D. 60.

boutique
A small fashionable store that is not part of a chain of stores.

These simple Neolithic huts were built more than 5,500 years ago.

The Romans used African elephants to frighten and trample their enemies.

Britons
The people of Great Britain.

Caxton, William (c. 1415–1492)
An English merchant and printer who was the first to print and publish books in English, in 1473.

Celts
A people from central Europe who settled in Great Britain in the 800s B.C.

Thames lightermen delivered paper to William Caxton's printing house.

chariot
A two-wheeled horse-drawn war cart used to carry soldiers.

Christian
Someone who follows the religion begun by Jesus of Nazareth (born 7–2 B.C.; died A.D. 26–36), and worships him as the son of God.

City (of London)
The original walled area that London occupied and, later, the financial and banking district.

civil war
A war between people of the same country.

conquest
The capture and rule of a country or city by its enemies, using force.

crusades
The campaigns in the A.D. 1000s–1200s by *Christian* soldiers to free the holy land of Palestine from Muslim rule.

cursus
A *Neolithic* avenue of two straight ditches and banks, probably used as part of a religious *ritual*.

customhouse
A building used for the collection of taxes on goods carried across a country's border.

daub
A mud coating for walls, smeared onto *wattle*.

Neolithic pots

drover
Someone who drives farm animals, usually to the marketplace in town.

East India Company
A British company formed in 1600 to trade with India that eventually grew to control India.

Edward IV (1442–1483)
The king of England from 1461. Edward's rule was broken for six months by a rebellion in 1470–1471.

Elizabeth I (1533–1603)
The queen of England and Ireland from 1558 until her death. Elizabeth's rule helped make her country wealthy and powerful.

epidemic
A serious outbreak of a disease in which many people get sick or die.

firebreak
An area deliberately cleared of anything that might burn in order to stop a fire from spreading.

Fleet (river)
A small river that runs into the River *Thames*, once used for dumping garbage, now hidden below-ground.

forum
The marketplace and central open space of a *Roman* town.

game
Wild birds and animals hunted for food.

George III (1738–1820)
The king of Great Britain from 1760 until his death. During George's reign, Great Britain's American settlers rebelled to form the United States.

gladiator
A slave trained to fight in combats staged in a *Roman amphitheater*.

Globe theater
A round wooden theater on *Bankside* where the *Lord Chamberlain's Men* performed.

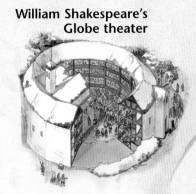
William Shakespeare's Globe theater

guild
A medieval organization in charge of a particular trade.

Iceni
A tribe of *Celts* who lived in what is now Norfolk and Suffolk in eastern England.

John, King (1167–1216)
The king of England from 1199 until his death in a *civil war*. Great Britain's rebelling barons forced John to sign the *Magna Carta*.

lead
A heavy gray metal that is soft and easy to shape.

lighterman
A sailor who ferries goods on rivers using a flat-bottomed barge.

Londinium
The *Roman* name for London.

London Bridge
The name for the first bridge to cross the River *Thames* in London and for all later bridges on roughly the same spot.

a Black Death burial pit

Lord Chamberlain's Men
The theater company of which *William Shakespeare* was a member.

Louis VIII (1187–1226)
The king of France who briefly ruled half of England around 1216.

Lundenwic
The name for London when the city was controlled by *Saxons* in the A.D. 600s and 700s.

Magna Carta
A document limiting the power of *King John*, which England's barons forced him to sign in 1215.

mason
A worker who cuts and lays the stones used to construct buildings.

Mediterranean
The region around the Mediterranean Sea, which separates southern Europe from North Africa.

migration
The movement of people between countries or continents.

a German Heinkel He III bomber from World War II

Mithraeum
A temple for the worship of *Mithras*.

Mithras
A Persian god of light and truth, worshiped by *Romans* in the first century B.C.

mods
Originally a nickname for followers of modern jazz, in the 1960s *mod* described people who dressed in designer clothes and danced to popular music.

monastery
The home and place of work and worship for monks, men who live simple lives devoted to God.

mosque
A place of worship for Muslims, people who follow the religion of Islam.

New Stone Age
An ancient period when people learned how to make finely polished stone tools.

Neolithic
See *New Stone Age*.

nomadic
Wandering, with no fixed home.

Normandy
A region of northern France.

Normans
A French people from *Normandy* who conquered England in the A.D. 1000s, led by *William the Conqueror*.

Palace of Westminster
The place where Great Britain's parliament meets and the home of England's kings from the A.D. 1000s to the 1500s.

Pepys, Samuel (1633–1703)
A naval officer who became famous for the diary he kept in London from 1660 to 1669.

pitch
A thick oily substance painted on walls and other surfaces to make them waterproof.

plague
A disease that spreads quickly and kills many people in a short time.

playwright
A person who writes plays.

pontoon
A temporary river bridge resting on boats or floats.

pop art
A style of art from the 1960s using strong colors and bold images, often based on advertising, news, or photographic images.

quay
A raised waterside area where ships load and unload their goods.

refugee
Someone who goes abroad to find protection from religious or political turmoil in their home country.

ritual
Special actions repeated in a strict order, often as part of a religious service or ceremony.

Romans
A people from the city of Rome who founded an empire that, by the 100s B.C., controlled England and much of Europe.

King Louis VIII traveled to London from France in 1216 and replaced the English king.

the White Tower
under construction

St. Paul's Cathedral
The largest and most important *Christian* church in the *City of London*.

Saxons
A German people who invaded Great Britain in the A.D. 400s and settled there.

Shakespeare, William (1564–1616)
An actor and theater manager in the *Lord Chamberlain's Men* who became Great Britain's (and the world's) most famous *playwright*.

shells

a British antiaircraft gun from World War II

Explosives fired from large guns.

Soho
A lively neighborhood of small streets in the center of London's West End and a popular spot for eating, drinking, and entertainment since the A.D. 1800s.

Southwark
A district of London, south of *London Bridge*.

stock exchange
A place where traders gamble on the future value of businesses and by doing so raise money for the expansion of those businesses.

synagogue
A temple of worship for Jews, people who follow the religion of Judaism.

Thames (river)
The large river that runs through London.

Tower of London
The castle built in the A.D. 1000s by the *Normans* in London's southeastern corner.

Tyburn
A place in west London traditionally used for public executions (punishment killings).

V-2
A missile fired at London from the European mainland by the Germans during *World War II*.

Victoria, Queen (1819–1901)
England's queen from 1837 until her death. Victoria reigned for longer than any English ruler before or since.

Vikings
Seafaring people who raided European ships and coastlines from their Scandinavian bases, from the A.D. 700s to the 1000s.

Walbrook Stream
A small river, now covered over, that once ran through the middle of the walled *City of London*.

wattle
A woven panel of twigs used in construction, often coated with *daub*.

Westminster Abbey
The main church of Westminster, once the place of worship for a *monastery* located there.

wharf
See *quay*.

White Tower
The original *Tower of London* and later the largest of several buildings together enclosed by walls and the River *Thames*.

William the Conqueror (c. 1028–1087)
Originally named William of *Normandy*, a *Norman* duke who conquered England in 1066 and became the country's king.

World War II (1939–1945)
A catastrophic six-year war in which Great Britain, the United States, and their military allies fought an alliance that included Germany, Italy, and Japan.

Wren, Christopher (1632–1723)
An English architect who designed a new *St. Paul's Cathedral* and many other churches after they were destroyed in the Great Fire of London in 1666.

In 1900, most London traffic was still drawn by horses—including large omnibuses.

Index

The last person to be executed in Tyburn, west London, was a highwayman named John Austin in 1783.

Searchlights scanned the London sky for bombers during the Blitz of World War II.

For Heidi and Simon

Consultant: Dr. Hugh Clout, Department of Geography, University College London

Additional consultancy: John Clark at the Museum of London; Dr. Richard Dennis,
Department of Geography, University College London; Maya Gabrielle and Gwilym Jones;
Paul Needham at the Scheide Library, Princeton University Library, Princeton, New Jersey.

Additional illustration work by Monica Favilli and Cecilia Scutti

KINGFISHER
LONDON & NEW YORK

Distributed in the U.S. by Macmillan, 175 Fifth Ave., New York, NY 10010
Distributed in Canada by H.B. Fenn and Company Ltd., 34 Nixon Road, Bolton, Ontario L7E 1W2

Library of Congress Cataloging-in-Publication Data
has been applied for.

ISBN: 978-0-7534-6255-3

Kingfisher books are available for special promotions and premiums. For details contact:
Special Markets Department, Macmillan, 175 Fifth Avenue, New York, NY 10010.

For more information, please visit www.kingfisherpublications.com

First American Edition June 2009
Printed in Taiwan
1 3 5 7 9 8 6 4 2
1TR/0209/SHE/CLSN(CLSN)/158MA/C

**Westminster was the home of
English rulers from the A.D. 1000s
until the early 1500s.**